Presentation by *BookLeaf Publishing*

Web: www.bookleafpub.com

E-mail: info@bookleafpub.com

ISBN: 9789358312201

First edition 2023

terrible poems to lay myself bare

Mistress Shilayla

BookLeaf Publishing

India | USA | UK

*To the Captain, with all dreams everlasting.
You're my favorite person in charge.*

ACKNOWLEDGEMENT

I came across a challenge. Write 21 poems in 21 days, and at the end have them bound into a small volume. Thanks to Bookleaf, for letting me try something different.

PREFACE

And did you get what
you wanted from this life, even so?
I did.
And what did you want?
To call myself beloved, to feel myself
beloved on the earth

– "Late Fragment" by Raymond Carver

tell me

tell me where the heck i stand
tell me your disappointments
tell me your insecurities
tell me your successes
tell me your jealousies
tell me your letdowns
tell me your anxieties
tell me your thoughts
tell me your dreams
tell me your failures
tell me your wishes
tell me your sorrow
tell me your beliefs
tell me your hopes
tell me your prides
tell me your wants
tell me your goals
tell me your fears
tell me your lust
tell me your life
tell me your joy
tell me your ire
tell me you
tell me
tell me
tell me
please

terrible poems

i write terrible poems because that's what lovers
do
when love is lost, when it's broken,
or when it's denied,
when hearts are forsaken,
when affection has died.

i write terrible poems because that's what lovers
do
to find a way out
of the nightmare around me,
of all of the doubt,
and the pain you can't see.

i write terrible poems for what else can i do
when everything everywhere reminds me of you.

there's no happy ending,
no "better this way,"
just dreams that are rending
and nothing's okay.

i can't seem to get anything on the right track
i write terrible poems 'cause you haven't come
back.

how to parent

every child is different
every one a challenge
no two respond the same
no matter what
parenting by a set of rules,
if this then that
doesn't work and never could
your daughter, my son,
and our baby girl
were all ours in the end
you have a wet towel, dad
i like your shirt
i'll love you even when you're old and bald
daddy is the silliest
mommy is the best
i like what you're eating too
and much cookies after that
baby under bili-lights
boy walks under water
girl runs into a bench
yes, that was your daughter
we did the best we could
to figure things out as we went.
mistakes are just mistakes
and they don't define our worthiness

we loved our kids
we wanted the best for them
we still do,
and that's what really matters.

can't let go

you fall in and out of love too easily,
i can never let go
it always would've gone this way i guess
you feeling trapped,
getting restless
holding all your frustrations inside
making me believe you had none
until you couldn't take it anymore,
and still couldn't tell me what was wrong
or why

you fall in and out of love so easily,
but what we had was real
as real as the tears on my cheeks,
as the breath in my chest
as the beat of my heart
and that's why I can't let go.

songs

our beautiful, dear daughter
is in her daddy's book
he says she's okay
but really he thinks she's great

making up sweet ditties
is what we always did
sometimes stole and changed them,
but the feelings were truly felt

who else will do this now
or appreciate our art
these words belong to us, love
no one else could understand

night moves

i rolled right out of bed the other day
that's never happened before
i could've really hurt myself
but your pillow broke my fall
even in the dark of night,
even nearly two years gone,
you're still protecting me, my love
still sheltering me from the storm

your instinct is to bear the brunt,
to take it on your back
to hold everything inside until
your veneer starts to crack
but i am here for you, my love
i'll gladly lighten your load
and carry it beside you
down the long and winding road

any maybe one day we will find
those loads have lessened on their own
like rocks falling surreptitiously throughout
the Shawshank Prison yard
until we find ourselves at last
on a stark white sandy beach
holding hands and staring out
at the crystal clear blue sea

forgotten memories

forgive and forget
how possible is that?
i've forgiven many things in life
but forgetting is not my forte
is that not an asset?
aren't we little more than the collection of our
memories?
a result of our experiences and what we glean
from them?

perhaps not.
i look at my mother,
who can remember to the exact second
her reaction time result
(as part of her driver's test at age 16)
almost 60 years ago,
but can't recall if i've met her boyfriend of two
years
or her housekeeper of ten
she stood not ten feet from her living room
fireplace
at Christmastime
one day after claiming to want to build a fire
and said in all seriousness
to my request that we do so
that she didn't have a fireplace

this woman is still my mother
yet she is not herself at all
a piece of her is missing,
gone forever
yet not gone at all
for she is still her,
still the woman who raised me
who taught me showtunes
and made me a feminist,
whose brilliant mind contributes
(at least in part)
to the smarter parts of mine

are we our memories or not?
does it matter what we hold onto?
do we have to remember it all?
or can the things that matter stay,
and those that don't fly away,
never to be seen again

for me, what matters
is i love you
and you have always loved me
and we could have a life together
by just moving forward
and forgetting the pains of the past

i feel like i've turned a corner

i've felt like this for many months
that now forgetting goes easily
when coupled with forgiveness
and I've already done both

make, take, come, try

make some noise
make me laugh
make my day
make me come
make it last

take your time
take me on
take five
take a load off
take a little piece of my heart

come here
come back
come on down
come on over
come, baby, come

try me
try again
try it, you'll like it
try your best
try a little tenderness

laid bare

can i lay myself bare
will you show me you care
is there anything there
anymore

will i sink? will i swim?
will things stop feeling grim?
will the sun be this dim
from now on?

is it wrong? is it right?
is there no end in sight?
can we turn on the light
and just talk?

can you look in my eye
and just tell me why
there was no goodbye
when you walked?

or are there still tears
while denying your fears
and discounting the years
of our life?

whichever you do,
i know what was true
and i will love you
for all time

i hope and i pray
you'll meet me halfway
and then maybe you'll stay
at long last

but even if we must part
i'll still have my art
where I pour out my heart
re: the past

song lyrics

I can't live without your love and affection
Baby, it's you – you're the one I want, you're
the one I need
If you're lost, you can look and you will find me
time after time
Whatever tomorrow brings, I'll be there with
open arms and open eyes, yeah
And the greatest miracle of all is how I need
you, and how you needed me too
I'll be there til the stars don't shine, til the
heavens burst, and the words don't rhyme

I get lost in your eyes
You lost more than that in my backseat, baby –
Buckle up, baby, it's a bumpy ride
Words can't say what love can do
I don't need no license, to sign on no line

You get the best of my love
You know it's true, I'm crazy for you
I just want your extra time and your … kiss
The chills that you spill up my back leave me
filled with satisfaction

I have died every day waiting for you

Say my name, sunshine through the rain
Without you i'm not okay, and without you i've
lost my way

Take my hand, take my whole life too, for I can't
help falling in love with you
All of me loves all of you, all your curves and
all your edges, all your perfect imperfections

True blue, baby, I love you

no goodbye

most goodbyes aren't goodbyes
most endings aren't ends
most leavings have some kind of return
what goes up must come down, after all
how, then, to cope when there are no more
chances
no sweet, stolen glances
as time just advances
along
some so longs are forever
some adieus don't come back
some farewells are the last of their lot
but i hope and i pray
to what god i can't say
that your going away
is not
come see me again
you're the best among men
please remember when
you loved me
don't let this be the end
i so miss my friend
please somehow mend
our family

i love you forever,
and maybe even longer than that.

end of life

when i come to the end of my days
i hope you're there holding my hand
telling me of your love
and that everything is going to be okay

if you're at the end before me
i hope to be at your side
holding your hand,
crying on your shoulder,
telling you how very much you're loved

let me lie down next to you
and apologize for all of my shortcomings
any time i didn't do right by you
let me hold you in my arms,
feel your breath under my cheek
as i listen to your heartbeat before it ends

i hope to be the first to go,
i hope you'll be there by me
i hope to hear you tell me you love me
one last time

hold my hand
cry on my shoulder

tell me you'll see me,
love me, and
kiss me in the next life
and everything will be okay

with love all this is possible

what went wrong,
by my hand and by yours
cannot be changed
instead we must shift focus
to lead us together
to the new possibilities that await
we can't fix the past,
but we can fix ourselves
we can fix each other
we can fix our relationship
with love, all this is possible
the ones we love the most
are the ones we wind up hurting
you hurt me and i hurt you
i forgave you
will you forgive me?
with love all this is possible
we loved bright like fire
we loved fierce like lions
we loved strong like steel
we loved deep as the sea
our love endures like time
let us not forsake
the gift the universe bestowed
with love all this is possible

meanderings

i lay myself bare
beaten down by despair
you're here but you're not here
you're there
so close but so far
i get in my car
my inability to leave
feels bizarre
but i sit and i stare
and still go nowhere
because knowing i failed you
i can't bear
where did it go wrong
our love was a song
perhaps I've been ruined
all along
or did you break us
throw us under the bus
because you've been known
to be self-traitorous
i must say i don't know
which neglected row
is the one that we
failed to hoe
i just know i love you

and that you love me too
no matter what else
that's still true

madness

wrong once again
said something dumb
mad at myself for being weak
mad at myself for being awkward
mad at myself for being useless
mad at you for believing it too
mad at you because I'm mad at me

this calls for a spreadsheet

label all your columns and your rows
map the trajectory of our life
with data over flowery prose
we were new kids
with the right stuff
and now our daughter
dreams of NASA
have you heard of it?
find the right function
make the math fit
confess your love in my bed
and again with a thrust
nothing like this has happened before
close your eyes and trust
in me, in you, in our blended lives
you disdain all your colleagues
who disdain their wives
filter them out and
follow your heart
you wanted this wedding
til death do we part
but first there were ups
and then there were downs
we needed to be frank
it turned us around

true love, he said, true love
you couldn't have a more noble cause
as loyal as she with her four tiny paws
a very cute head
and sentry by your seat
when she sits you can see
her weird E.T. feet
a boy we named Froley
and the girl was Bazooka
gumming things up
like kids always do
then the miracle astronaut
threw us for a loop
if then plus that
put the equation in brackets
we were a family
in matched puffer jackets
then things went downhill
in mindy, body and soul
and not just for me
you too took a toll
i wish i had seen
or been made to understand
that your ring came like
a weight on your hand
maybe just indulge
in a flirtation or two
get back your old mojo
like the man you're used to

be like your old self
the troublemaker, the thug
sweep all your guilt
right under the rug
until it eats you up inside
and you can no longer breathe
unwilling to face me
through the tangled weave
is there a doctor who
can mend these wounds
you say no for me
i don't get to choose
now i can't reach you
you've sailed your ship
is there an aqueous transmission
to curtail your trip?
drag me to hell
the race hasn't started
if x = 33
i'm left brokenhearted
perhaps a pivot table
can analyze our findings
around the world comes back again
i seek you with glad tidings
i want to talk things over
in your shoes i'll walk a mile
would you do the same for me
would you love to see me smile
once again forevermore

our memories free of bile
because death cannot stop true love
only delay it for a while
resort your spreadsheet
tell me what does it say
i'm dying to not leave our
love life this way

empty

across the room
i search for you
i know you should be here
but you haven't graced these halls
in far too long
your weight has not imprinted on our bed in
months and months
our house is a wasteland,
falling into ruin without our love to make it
whole
my soul is cold and barren
an empty void without its other half
i'm out of time
out of chances
out of ideas
out of hope

i hate her (me)

i hate the woman
you've turned me into
i hate her anger and her bitterness
i hate how raw her pain is,
and how it makes her lash out viciously
i hate that she can't be mad or sad or lost
without being shamed for not be fine
i hate how you ignore her
because it only makes her hurt worse
i hate how you disdain her
because she never deserved anything
but your sorrow, your regret, your apology
i hate how she's forced to be strong,
to suck it up,
to pretend like it's just another day
every day that you tear her heart open
you may be able to shut off your feelings,
to forget, to deny, to hide,
but she can't,
she has no switch for that,
she's not a robot or a cold fish
and i hate her every day for it

wrong idea

i had the wrong idea
about how things went down
about the way you felt
about the life we had
i had the wrong idea
about the love we shared
because it's over now
because you're a
long time gone
i never thought I had it wrong
but i must've all the same
i must've had the wrong idea
because everything is ruined
everything is wrong
i must've had the wrong idea
or else why aren't you here?
why else are all my words mistakes
and all my actions failed?
i must've been wrong all along
or else you'd not have bailed

broken

in the rush to replace me
to forget me
and deny me
you've made the same mistakes
you disdained me for
the same entanglement
the same dependence
the same responsibility
the same obligations
break me off
i don't grow back
i just stay broken
raw and ragged
scabbed and bloody
frayed and worn

rambling (two year remix)

i thought i had a friend,
but was he just fair weather?
i thought i had a lover,
but he let his love run cold
he spent his love on someone else
leaving not enough for me
not enough, not enough.
i thought my heart was safe with him,
i thought his heart was mine,
but he squirreled it away in the night.

he wouldn't let me see him,
he wouldn't let me know him.
he never trusted me to love him exactly as he
was.
always hedging who he was and what he
thought,
never letting all of himself free.

scared he couldn't face me,
he closed himself off behind walls
until he couldn't breathe within the confines of
his prison
and he sought his solace elsewhere.
now all the lies have gone too long
and what's been found feels easier to hold onto

he would've kept our family strong,
if i hadn't found him out,
but now the jig is up, and
one lie's been uncovered.
so cut and run is the only choice,
or else he'd have to face his ills,
and lay his body bare.
no more lying and no more running
it terrifies him to his core.

so he hurts me and he scorns me,
sses his words and mind to thrash against me,
tries to make me hate him, make me leave him,
make me curse the day i met him.
i can see his pain that he won't name,
and i didn't understand at first
i wasn't wrong about his love.
i know i wasn't. i feel it in my bones.
so how did everything go wrong?

put your fears away, my love.
put your trust in me.
i can be the stronger one,
but not if you decide to leave.
i won't survive this break from you
i can't go through the pain.
don't ask it of me, i beg of you.
don't make this our last refrain.

scold me and chastise me
call me all the cussing names
punish me for disobeying
for acting without permission
and never notice that you've
made me less than you
subordinate
submissive
in ways you never wanted before

i'm not a poet,
or not a good one, still
but prose is too hard to conquer when my
words are scarce and scattered
when my heart is pounding through my chest
and
every fiber hurts
when my eyes feel sore and red from weeping
and my breath comes in soft bursts
what have you done to us, my love?
what are you doing to me?
why don't you care about our lives, our kids, our
history?

stop pushing me away, my love.
stop forcing me to crumble.
stop asking me to think of you
in the worst light imaginable.

stop thinking of me that way in turn.
tell me everything, my love.
get it off your chest.
spill your secrets, confess your sins
and tear your walls away.
at least then you would know if
i would've loved you anyway.

regret me, mourn me, miss me, dear.
take this to your grave.
see this as the biggest error
that you've ever made.
i see your obstinance
i see your fear and anger.
i see your pain and misery
and i want to make it better.

but what's made better for me?
anything? not really.
i cannot face that pain again.
i'm literally not able.
i'm falling, failing, breaking daily
i'm alone and lonely
hated and berated
everything's just getting worse,
and nobody can save me.
i long for a sweet release
all i do is misbehave

www.ingramcontent.com/pod-product-compliance
Lightning Source LLC
La Vergne TN
LVHW051241200726
843510LV00011B/1637